First English edition in 2018

Hamad bin Khalifa University Press
P O Box 5825
Doha, Qatar

www.hbkupress.com

First published in English in 2017 as A *Recipe for home*

Copyright © Ghenwa Yehia, 2018

All rights reserved.

No part of this publication may be reproduced or transmitted in any form or by any means, electronic or mechanical, including photocopying, recording, or any information storage or retrieval system, without prior permission in writing from the publishers.

No responsibility for loss caused to any individual or organization acting on or refraining from action as a result of the material in this publication can be accepted by HBKU Press or the author.

ISBN: 978-9927119835

Printed and bound in Doha, Qatar by Al Jazeera Printing Press Co. L.L.C.

Qatar National Library Cataloging-in-Publication (CIP)

Yehia, Ghenwa, author.

 A recipe for home / by Ghenwa Yehia ; illustration by Inna Ogando. – First English edition. - Doha : Hamad Bin Khalifa University Press, 2018.

   Pages ; cm

ISBN : 978-9927-119-83-5

1. Cooking -- Juvenile stories. 2. Recipes -- Juvenile stories. I. Ogando, Inna, illustrator. II. Title.

TX652.5.Y44 2018

641.5 – dc23

201726189665

A Recipe for Home

By: Ghenwa Yehia
Illustrations by: Inna Ogando

Layan and her friends were walking home from school one day, when her stomach suddenly rumbled as she spied the plump dates at the tops of the trees.

"I'm so hungry!" she exclaimed. Her friends nodded in agreement.

"I've got the best idea," said Layan.

"Let's have a picnic; a potluck picnic! Everyone can bring their favourite food from home and we can all share. It will be a feast!"

Joanna's face lit up at the mention of food.

"I can bring fish and chips!" she yelled.

"My mum takes the slipperiest, slimiest fish and dips it into a gooey, sticky batter.

"I get to drop it into the pot of hot oil, but I have to jump back because it explodes with bubbles. It comes out golden brown and it makes a big CRUNCH when you bite into it."

"Well, have you ever tried raw fish?" Haruko piped in.

"Father puts it in sushi. Sushi is a roll made with vinegar-soaked rice, vegetables and raw fish wrapped in seaweed.

"Father is responsible for cutting up the vegetables and fish into thin slices. Then, I lay the seaweed on the sushi mat that I use to make rolls topped off with the rice, vegetables and fish."

"That sounds cool!" said Gia.

"My *nonna* is visiting us. I can see if she can make us some of her traditional *spaghetti alla bolognese*.

"Nonna and I make the spaghetti by mixing flour and eggs, and then pounding and stretching and rolling the dough until it's just right.

"Then she cuts it into long, thin ropes and puts it into a pot of boiling water to cook.

"When it's ready, my *nonna* piles the spaghetti on a plate and she tops it off with bright red tomato sauce and juicy meatballs."

"Hmm..." thought Layan aloud.

"I could bring my Grandma Jo's oatmeal chocolate chip cookies. When I travelled to visit her on winter break, Grandma Jo taught me the recipe.

"Butter, sugar, flour, eggs, oats and chocolate chips. Grandma let me mix together the tough batter, which was kind of hard, but the cookies always turned out warm and soft and delicious."

"Or…" she continued,
"I could bring *tabouli*."

"In the summer, Teta Susu and I would make it every day with lunch. We picked the parsley, tomatoes, mint and green onions right from Teta's vegetable garden, in the backyard.

"Then Teta would chop them up and mix in some dried, cracked wheat called burghul.

"I squeezed the lemons, and added olive oil and salt for the tangy sauce and it was ready to eat."

"That seems like a lot of work," Joanna interrupted.

"Well, I guess I could just ask my mom and dad to pick up some *machbous* for the picnic," answered Layan.

"What's that?" asked Haruko.

"It's a flavoured rice made with many spices and piled high with tender, juicy meat.

"You're supposed to eat it using only three fingers on your right hand," Layan explained.

"My family and I always eat *machbous* on Fridays at the restaurant around the corner from our house."

"Cool!" said Gia

At that, the friends went their separate ways and agreed to meet at the park at five o'clock.

When Layan got home, she explained to her mom that her friends had easily decided what special food to bring to the potluck picnic.

They would each bring a dish that they made with someone they love, and was something that made them feel at home.

"For me, home means so many things," Layan explained.

"Sharing cookies with Grandma Jo when it's cold and snowing outside...

"... the adventure of making Teta Susu's tabouli from the garden...

"... and Friday nights at the restaurant with my brothers all feel like home."

"It seems like a difficult choice," empathised Layan's mom.

"It is!" cried Layan.

"How can I pick just one special food to bring to the potluck when all of these foods remind me of home and of the people that I love?"

"Well, I think," said Layan's mom, "that home is not a place, or a food, or a country; these things only represent home.

"Home is a feeling.

"And wherever you are surrounded by the people you love, doing something you love, that is home."

"Well then, I want to share a special food from each one of the places that feels like home!" Layan said excitedly.

And with that, she set off chopping and mixing, whipping and pouring, and boiling and baking.